MOMENTS THAT MATTER

MOMENTS THAT MATTER

ROBERT MARTINEAU

Bishop of Blackburn

London
SPCK

First published 1976
SPCK
Holy Trinity Church
Marylebone Road
London NW1 4DU

Printed in Great Britain
Bocardo & Church Army Press Ltd
Cowley, Oxford

84234

ISBN 0 281 02920 2

CONTENTS

CONTENTS

PREFACE

There are moments in life when people who are not regular worshippers look to the Church for help. At the birth of a child, most parents ask for their child to be baptized; about half the children baptized in the Church of England are confirmed, though a much smaller proportion become regular worshippers. Many people come to be married in Church, who have little connection with its worshipping life. The vicar is expected to visit the sick, to be available in time of trouble and, above all, to bury the dead.

This book, following the theme of a series of Teaching Missions in parishes both at home and abroad, is an attempt to show how these moments in life are occasions when we can gain special insights into Christian truth. They can be moments of vision as well as of need, of insight as well as of decision. The fact that so many people are in touch with the Church at these moments, and then so quickly lose that contact, implies that they did not catch the vision or grasp the truth.

Behind all that is written here lies the belief that Jesus Christ shared our frail human life and invites us to share his risen and victorious life. Thus not only are these great moments occasions when it is easier to gain special insights into Christian truth, they are moments when some particular strength or gift of God is made available. They are moments which matter to us; they are moments which matter to God.

This book was written initially in connection with the Jubilee of the Diocese of Blackburn, in the hope that it would help the people of the diocese to understand their faith. I am grateful to the S.P.C.K. for their readiness to make the book more widely available.

ROBERT MARTINEAU

1

CHILDREN OF GOD

'Now are we the sons of God, and it doth not yet appear what we shall be' (1 John 3.2). The writer does not explain how we become sons of God, but he is quite clear that it makes such a difference to a person that he contrasts the children of God with the children of the devil (1 John 3.10). The difference is as great as that between light and darkness, as between truth and lies, as between love and hatred, as between life and death. Our status as children of God is a gift of God, bestowed on us out of the overflowing love of God; it is for the Christian to respond by loving God and by loving his brother, and by acknowledging Jesus to be the Christ, the Son of God. Because we are sons of God, we can call God 'Father', even though St Paul describes our sonship as being by adoption. Jesus indeed taught his disciples to address God as 'Father' when they prayed. With the solitary exception of the word from the cross (*Eli, Eli, lama sabachtani*), Jesus always himself addressed God as Father. The sonship that he possessed, he desired to share with us. Thus, after the resurrection he is reported as saying to Mary Magdalene, 'Go to my brethren and say unto them, I ascend unto my Father and your Father, and to my God and your God.'

'God sent his Son . . . that we might receive the adoption of sons' (Gal. 4.4-5). We respond by faith and love and obedience. Outwardly, the response from the very earliest time included baptism, which would bring with it the gift of the Holy Spirit (Acts 2.38). Thus, at the very least, baptism is the ceremony which marks the start of a person's life as a child of God. The difference between that life and our natural life in the world is such that Jesus describes it as being 'born again'. Some of the characteristics of birth are singularly relevant with regard to the beginning of new life in Christ. In respect of earthly human birth, the initiative is not of the child but of the parents. Sonship is a status given to a child by his parents; indeed, his very existence is the consequence of their action. Ideally, the child is born because his parents wanted him and is loved because he is theirs. So in our coming to sonship of God, the initiative is with God. We become children of God because our heavenly Father wants us as his children, and he loves us not because we are good but because he is. Again ideally, when Christian parents bring their earthly child to baptism, they are believing that as they have given their child earthly life, so God their Father desires their child as his child and wants to give him eternal life. Thus, they are not afraid to bring their infant to baptism long before he can possibly know the difference between right and wrong, between truth and falsehood, or before he can have any knowledge of Jesus Christ the unique Son of God. They know their child to be their own, and they bring him up to know them as his parents. They love him and hope that he will grow up to love them in return. They believe God loves him more than any earthly father can, and they will bring him up in such a way that they hope he will come to know and love God as his Father.

Parental love and care were used by Jesus as an illustration of God's love for us. 'What man is there of you whom if his son ask bread will give him a stone? Or if he ask a fish will he give him a serpent? If ye then, being evil, know how to give good gifts unto your children, how much more shall your Father which is in heaven give good things to them that ask him?' Earthly parents give what is good for their child long before he asks for it or is capable of knowing the meaning of gratitude. They give because they love and because they know their child needs food and warmth, protection and care, and so many other expressions of love. In due course they will teach their child to say 'Please' and 'Thank you', and so to learn the meaning of dependence and gratitude. Because they themselves are dependent upon God and grateful to him, they will bring up their child in the hope that he will realize these things for himself. But they know that God will not withhold his gifts because of their ingratitude. (The nine ungrateful lepers were healed as well as the one who returned to give thanks.)

Baptism is the beginning of new life in Christ. Neither cleansing nor burial exhausts the symbolism of baptism. There is the signing or sealing, which is linked in the New Testament with the giving of the Spirit. More correctly, it might be described as the beginning of the giving of the Spirit. (The analogy of the payment of a deposit is almost exact.) The baptism service as we have it makes this signing a separate action from the pouring of water. The newly-baptized is signed with the sign of the cross in token that he shall never be ashamed to confess the faith of Christ crucified but manfully shall fight under his banner against sin, the world and the devil, and continue Christ's faithful soldier and servant to his life's end. The newly-baptized is marked as belonging to Christ. It would be stretching credulity beyond all limits to separate the actual baptism — sharing the death and risen life of Christ — from the signing with the sign of the Cross — the assurance of the giving of the Spirit. All are parts of one act of initiation into Christ and life in the Spirit.

Further, this new life is life in the Body of Christ, and incorporation into the Body is inseparably linked with baptism. This incorporation has its effect not only on the new member of Christ but also on the Body. Baptism thus not only affects the person baptized but also affects the Church, which has to be ready to welcome the new member and accept him into its life. In theory (and in the case of private baptism because of emergency, in practice) baptism and reception by the Church into its membership and fellowship can be treated as two actions, but neither can be complete without the other. Thus, the plea that baptism should take place at a main service of the Church is not only for the sake of the newly-baptized and his family, but as much for the sake of the Church, which now has an additional responsi-bility. The analogy with birth into the human domestic family is almost exact. The newly-born becomes a member of the family by birth, inheriting brothers and sisters and other relations; similarly they welcome their new brother and acquire a new responsibility as a result. To some extent in the family-fellowship of the Body of Christ it is the parents and godparents who exercise this responsibility on behalf of the whole Church, but there is a very real sense in which it can be said that each baptism affects not only the newly-baptized but also the whole Church.

The significance of all these things derives from the Christian understanding of the fatherhood of God. God's fatherhood takes on new meaning as a result of the incarnation in Jesus Christ. He took our nature upon him, sharing our life, and invites us to share his life. The birth of Jesus was an event not only with theological significance, described in the Athanasian Creed as God taking manhood into himself, but also an event which affected the character of the human race. The human race now contained Jesus as a member and because of that fact was wholly transformed in character. The word 'fatherhood' in the sense in which it applies to 'the Father of our Lord Jesus Christ' now applies to the whole human race at least as a possibility. For if it is the will of God that all men should be saved, it is his will that all men should come to know Christ and share his life. Because of the incarnation, men are offered a new status in relation to God, and this status belongs to the realm of the eternal.

This status is not limited by space and time, in the way that earthly family relationships are so limited. There is no ground for believing that the earthly family relationships have any significance in any 'life after death'. Indeed, the reply of our Lord to the Sadducees, who posed the conundrum about a woman who had married seven brothers in turn, is, to say the least, an indication to the contrary (Mark 12.18-27). Further, the very conundrum is a reminder that even earthly family relationships can and do change. Thus ideally, two persons who are baptized have something in common which is more abiding and of greater significance than anything they have in common with one another or with anyone else according to the flesh. Equally, they have something in common which is of (infinitely) greater significance than any differences they have between them according to the flesh. Thus a black child, a coloured child, and a white child baptized (not necessarily at the same service) into the Body of Christ have a common relationship with the Father and therefore with one another, a status which no structure of separate development can ultimately affect. The structures of society may affect their appreciation of this status, just as the divisions of the Church affect our own appreciation of our unity in Christ with baptized persons of other traditions. At the present time the significance of the baptismal unity of Christian people within a divided Church is being more and more recognized. The quest for a united Church is less directed towards the formation of a structure into which Christians hitherto separated may find themselves included and is more directed to removing those inessential things which hinder the growth in the one Body of those who have been made members of Christ in the one baptism.

In practice, these ideas are not readily in the minds of those who bring their children to their local Church to be baptized, or christened, as they commonly describe it. As far as they are concerned, the theologians can go on disputing. They have a belief that it is a right thing to do for the child's sake, even though they themselves may have given up any practice of public worship or any other expression of their own identification with the Church. The fact that over half of all children baptized in the Church of England are not confirmed suggests that any link between baptism and a lively faith in Jesus Christ is just not present in the minds of very many people. The fact that just under half do come forward for Confirmation suggests that this link does exist in the minds of many other people. Various commissions have met and reported on this confused situation. The subject can be guaranteed to provide a lively debate in almost any group of parish priests.

Part of the difficulty lies in too much concentration on what happens to the child, how baptism, reception into the Church, faith in Christ on the child's part, and his eventual declaration of that faith and of resolve to live a Christian life are linked together. There is too little concentration on what happens to the Body of Christ every time there is a baptism, the effect of the reception of the newly-baptized on the Church which does the receiving, the responsibility of the company of the faithful to take steps to share their faith with the baptized and to incorporate him in their fellowship so that they may live out the Christian life in fellowship with one another in Christ. The baptism service in the Methodist Church recognizes this point when the minister asks the congregation, 'Will you endeavour so to maintain here a fellowship of worship and service in the Church that (this child) may grow up in the knowledge and love of God and of his Son Jesus Christ our Lord?'

It may take at least a generation for the change of emphasis from the effect of baptism on the child to the effect of baptism on the Church, both theologically and pastorally, to result in a change of baptismal practice and adequate pastoral after-care by priest and congregation, but for the sake of the Church the change must take place. (Some interesting theological and pastoral questions affecting the unity of the Church arise, for instance, when one considers what responsibility the Anglican Church has towards infants baptized in the Methodist Church and vice versa.) If this change of emphasis were effected, there would be less talk of parental irresponsibility towards the Church on behalf of their children. There would be more recognition of the Church's irresponsible neglect of those who in baptism were welcomed into the one Body of Christ, for whom it is God's will that they come to a knowledge and love of Jesus Christ.

One of the characteristics of the perfect fatherhood of God to which infant baptism bears witness is that God's love for the child is not conditional upon the child's response, or even upon the child's ability to respond. Again, the analogy of earthly family life is strong. Parents do not reject their child just because it happens to be handicapped, mentally or physically. Indeed, the greater dependence of the child on his parents may make the expression of their love in time and trouble seem to the outsider to be all the greater. Nor do earthly parents give up loving their child because he is rebellious or unloving in return. In the same way, there are no limits to the unconditional love of God either in its endurance or in its embrace. The full significance of this cannot be grasped apart from an understanding of the place of the cross in regard to the forgiveness of sin. Though the parents of children brought to baptism probably do not realize this, the idea of the forgiveness of sins is part of the meaning of baptism in that the child is made a member of a society of forgiven sinners. What they can more readily grasp is that the child is marked (with the sign of the cross) as belonging to God and that, whatever else happens, God will go on loving his own child. In a mobile society, this fact becomes more important. When the earthly family moves to a new area, they and their children belong of right to the Church there as they did to the Church in the place from which they came. Baptism is one witness to the fact that the fatherhood of God is limited neither by time nor by geography.

Note on the Symbolism of Baptism

The symbolism of baptism is related to more than one image in the New Testament, and there is no direct and simple teaching by Jesus about its significance. There is the command described in the closing verses of St Matthew's Gospel, but no symbolic meaning is attached. The baptism of John was the outward sign of washing away the sinful past and starting again clean. The symbolism of washing clean is familiar in the Old Testament, though the word from which baptism derives is not commonly used; purification is a more common image. In washing, as in purification (which could be 'by fire'), what is imperfect and unworthy and unwanted is removed, so that the vessel or the person may be fit for use by God. Before making an offering to God, not only must the offering be

B

without blemish, but the offerer must be clean. Clearly, however, the early Church understood Christian baptism as having more meaning than cleansing. It was seen as an outward sign of burial and rising to new life. Thus, St Paul speaks of being buried with Christ by baptism into his death (Rom. 6.4) — that as he was raised again so we should also begin a new life. Earthly physical life cannot escape the death of the body; Christ came and shared our earthly nature, including death. Christ, however, overcame death and was raised to new life which death cannot touch (Rom. 6.9).

Baptism in this light is a sign of our sharing in that life of Christ which has passed through death into something new. The idea of the beginning of new life in Christ is probably easier to grasp than the significance of burial with Christ. Thus, at the end of the long dry season, I heard an African priest in Bloemfontein speaking about baptism. Pointing to the dark brown earth, he said that when God gave rain it would all spring into new life. The illustration may not be biblical; but its significance would not have been lost on his hearers.

2

GROWING UP IN THE FAMILY OF GOD

Confirmation, as practised at present, has two aspects. It is the occasion when a child is admitted to the privilege of being able to receive Holy Communion. It is also the occasion when an act of commitment is publicly declared, in the form of a renewal of his baptismal promises. Privilege and responsibility go hand in hand, which is quite right. Those who lay greater emphasis on the aspect of the privilege press for Confirmation at an early age, so long as the child is able to grasp the nature of the privilege. Those who lay greater emphasis on the aspect of commitment press for Confirmation at a later age, so that the act of commitment may be as mature as possible. There is no happy mean. As at present practised, preparation for Confirmation covers both those aspects. There is teaching about the meaning of Holy Communion and the privilege of being able to share in receiving it; the understanding both of that meaning and of that privilege will grow by experience more and more within the context of sharing in the Holy Communion. There is also teaching about the nature of commitment to Christ and the Christian life. Those about to be confirmed learn something of the meaning of their responsibility within the family of God, and they will go on learning by experience more and more.

Privilege and responsibility are characteristics of membership of the family of God. No one is good enough to deserve the privileges received within the family of God; equally no one is mature enough to make a complete act of commitment to Christ, or to understand the full meaning of such an act. Both these things are parts of an ongoing process. Just as the privileges are renewed again and again by God, so the act of commitment needs to be renewed again and again by man. This is to be expected from the nature of the promise itself, even though there must be a definite act of decision at some point. When Jesus called his disciples and said, 'Follow me', there was a moment of decision; the sequence of events throughout his ministry leading eventually to his trial and death called for continual renewal of the decision to go with Jesus and stand by him. Evidently in the Garden of Gethsemane they forsook him and fled, only to be strengthened by his risen presence and recommissioned in his service after the resurrection.

In normal human society, other than in a family, privilege is the reward of service. Privilege may take the form of certain rights which are not shared by other people, such as an extra week's holiday entitlement or a reserved place for one's car, or it may be the power to buy more than others because of a higher salary. The worldly way is to expect work or service first and to give privilege as a consequence. The world ideally works on a system of merit. A family reverses such a system. In a family, a child is born with all the privilege (or handicap) which membership of that family brings, and as the child grows to maturity he learns to accept the responsibilities which his privilege entails. The teaching of Jesus is that God sees and treats mankind as a family, and privilege precedes our acceptance of responsibility. The realm of grace is fundamentally different from that of merit. All the grace of God is available irrespective of the gratitude or moral rectitude of his creatures; such response as we give is a response to his goodness. This property of the family of God is so difficult to grasp that we easily slip into the way of the world and expect a pledge of loyalty before privileges may be received, penitence before forgiveness, instead of the other way round. It remains, however, that while in the world service brings privilege and in a family privilege carries with it responsibility, yet in either system the two go hand in hand.

In the new Service of Confirmation (Series 2), the decision declared by each candidate is that he turns to Christ, repents of his sins, and renounces evil. Here there is an offering of one's whole self including past, present, and future. Repentance of sin relates to the past, renouncing evil and turning to Christ relate to the future starting from now. Turning to Christ implies allowing him to be Lord of our lives. This means, among other things, that when we make decisions and plan the purpose of our lives and the use of our time and our money, we are controlled by what he wants us to do. This, of course, means finding out what he does want us to do, and the first and foremost way of doing this is through a prayerful and intelligent reading of the Bible and particularly the Gospels. I say our reading must be both prayerful and intelligent. Clearly, we must take trouble to find out the meaning of a passage and to see it in its context, for the Bible contains all kinds of passages — poetry, drama, parables, direct narrative, prayer, meditation, etc. — and it is very important to know what kind of passage we are reading. The more trouble we are prepared to take to find out the context and meaning of what we read in the Bible, the richer will be its message to us. It is also true that the more willing we are to let Christ be the Lord of our life, the more meaning we shall find in even such apparently simple sayings as the Beatitudes. No one can fully understand the Scripture unless he is prepared to live by it. First and foremost, then, if we want to know what Christ wants to say to us, we ask him who is the Word, who was made flesh, to enlighten us through the words of Scripture.

As we read the words of Jesus in the Gospels, we find him sometimes speaking to people in general, sometimes to his followers, and sometimes to one individual in particular. What he said to one individual could well be different from what he said to another; to one he said, 'Go and tell what God has done for you', to another he said, 'See thou tell no one.' If we count ourselves as followers of Jesus, then what he said to his followers (as distinct from what he said to the world at large) will apply directly to us. It was, for instance, to his followers in particular that he said, 'Whosoever would be great among you must be servant.' It is by trying to put this into practice within the fellowship of Christ's followers that we learn more of the depth of its meaning.

In addition to the will of God expressed in the Gospels, either to mankind in general or to the followers of Christ, there is his particular will for each individual which comes to us in two principal ways. Partly it dawns on us as we say our prayers. For instance, if we pray, 'Forgive us our trespasses as we

forgive those who trespass against us', and then pause
to consider whether there is someone whom we ought
to forgive more than we have done, God can and does
use the occasion to speak to us. Again, if we pray,
'Thy will be done' and then realize that we are living
our lives to please ourselves in some area of concern,
then God can and does use the occasion to make us
realize how we can devote more of our time and attention to serve others for his sake. In response, we pray
that he will make the way clearer. The other principal
way in which God makes his particular will known to
us is through the people we meet. Clearly, it calls for
prayerful sensitivity on our part to distinguish between
our own wishful thinking (or the earthly and selfish
opinions of others) and the will of God which he is
trying to use others to convey. By no means does it
always happen that the person being so used is aware
of the fact; indeed, the contrary is often the case, and
it comes as a complete surprise when years afterwards one learns that something one has said has
made all the difference to the direction or meaning of
another's life. God takes one person and uses him to
say something to another which strikes home.

In these and other ways God guides those who are
seeking his guidance. Turning to Christ means 'looking
unto Jesus' to pay attention to him, learning more
and more what sort of people he expects his followers
to become and what sort of response he expects them
to make. When by the grace of God we do discern his
guidance, we find we need more inward strength than
we have by nature to follow that guidance. This leads
us to a second aspect of Confirmation, that of God's
gift of inward, spiritual strength. In Confirmation, we

B2

ask for the protecting power of God's spirit. The
action of the bishop in laying his hands on the head of
each person to be confirmed is accompanied by the
prayer that God will defend that particular child of
God, daily increase his Holy Spirit in him, and keep
him his for ever. This is certainly a prayer that we can
trust God to answer, for those things are part of the
express will of God revealed by Christ; indeed, it is
another way of saying, 'Thy will be done.'

The Christian life calls for more courage than we
have by nature; it calls for more humility and more
endurance, and more of many other qualities also,
than we have by nature. But we can trust the promise
of Jesus that God will give us these things, and all
other good things which we need, if we really want
them and if we ask him. In particular, he will give us
strength in time of temptation, when we are tempted
to shirk our duty because we are lazy, or answer back
sharply through bad temper, or not apologize through
pride, and so on. It is one thing to know what is the
right thing to do (this itself being a gift of God) but
quite another thing to have the strength of spirit to do
it, and to do it in a charitable way. But this is just
what God wants us to have. God will not let us be
tempted beyond what we are able, but when we are
tempted will provide the means by which we are able
to bear it. We can do all things through Christ who
strengthens us. We must not only seek but be ready to
receive and accept his strength. Just as God does not
give us guidance for the whole of life all on one day,
no more does he give us on one day all the spiritual
strength we shall need for life. Day by day, week by
week throughout the years, we need to wait upon the

Lord who will renew our strength, not least through the Holy Communion.

Finally, Confirmation is an activity of the Church, the family of God. Much of the strength which is asked for in Confirmation is given through the Body of Christ. In baptism we become members of that Body and in Confirmation we openly accept the responsibility which our membership entails. Membership of the Body means that we never have to be followers of Christ all on our own; equally, we shall lose the benefit of the fellowship if we try to follow Christ on our own. The Bible speaks of the fellowship of the Spirit; we might almost call it 'togetherness in Christ'. This is why sharing in Holy Communion and in the ongoing life of the Church as a whole is so very important. We come to Communion and hold out our hands for the bread of life, and in a way beyond human description the life that was given for us is given to us. It is also given to our next-door neighbour, the person kneeling beside us. We share a common life in Christ. This means that if we accept our responsibilities as members of his Body, Christ will use us as a means by which his strength is given to other members. If our prayers for those who are being confirmed are genuine, God will use us to answer those prayers. God will give them some of the strength and some of the guidance that we have asked him to give them — through us. Our loyalty to Christ will help them to be loyal to him; our sharing in Communion will help it to mean more to them. We and they will all grow more Christlike, and all become spiritually stronger, as we stay together in the Body. Not only are they helped by our faithfulness, but we are helped by theirs.

3

CHRISTIAN MARRIAGE AND THE
MEANING OF LOVE

In looking at Christian marriage, it is necessary and important to repeat what is the purpose of this book. Our aim is to see how the events of human life are occasions from which we can gain insights into Christian truth, and occasions for which some special grace of God is available. Thus in thinking about Christian marriage I have no desire either to try to pronounce theologically upon its nature or to discuss the rights and wrongs of a second marriage when a first marriage has broken down. In the Marriage Service, however, there are some things which are assumed rather than stated which point to a Christian understanding of marriage and to the ways of God.

In the first place, the Service rests on an assumption that marriage is part of God's will for the couple, a joy and an adventure into which he is leading them. The fact that marriage is part of God's design for mankind is explicitly stated. Marriage was 'instituted of God himself', for the sake of any children, for the sake of society, and for the sake of the partners to the marriage themselves. At once we find that this assumption is as much about God as it is about marriage. Marriage cannot be part of God's plan for mankind unless God has a plan for mankind. In coming to church to be married (unless the occasion is a mere formality), the couple believe that God is concerned not just about marriage and mankind in general but about this particular marriage and themselves as a particular couple. It would be overstating the position to declare that God had all along designed that Mary and George should meet, fall in love, and marry, and that his will would have been thwarted if either (and presumably both, therefore!) had met and married someone else. But by the time the couple have arrived at church for the wedding, they believe they are doing the right thing in God's sight; that is, they are doing what is now God's will for them and they are ready to ask God to help them build their marriage into what he would like it to be, infinitely better than it would be otherwise.

Secondly, the Marriage Service assumes that the partners are ready and willing to share everything; they share their earthly possessions, they will share their home and their bodies. He gives himself wholly to her, and she gives herself to him, with the whole of his past and his future. This giving and taking is without condition or qualification, and in most modern forms of the Marriage Service, on precisely equal terms except that the name of the new family unit comes from the man's side. This complete and absolute sharing enables the two individuals to become a new unit. The creation of this new unit is as much the work of God as the children of the union are the gift of God, even though all the processes leading up to the birth are human. By the pledge of unconditional love which each gives to the other, the couple enable a bond to be forged between them which is of God. It is this that helps them to understand the third assumption about the Marriage Service, namely, that while in the eyes of the law and of the Church they marry one another, yet they themselves believe that God is doing something in them and to them. All the actions and words are human, and witnessed by men and women at a time and in a place chosen by the couple, with a ring and a certificate in green print to show for it; but God takes all these things and lifts them above the earthly level and fills them with a meaning which belongs to the realm of the eternal.

In the Marriage Service, this has three aspects: its significance for any children, for society, and for the couple themselves. It would certainly be possible to devise and organize a society in which family life as we know it had little or no place. The Christian and Jewish tradition is that marriage and family life are ingredients of human society as God meant it to be; that which contributes to the stability of home and family is good, and that which tends to disrupt it is evil. For the sake of any children, the importance of this is even greater as well as being more obvious. The Christian believes that all men are meant to know that they are children of God, their Father in heaven. Christian parents have the prime responsibility of helping their own children to know this for themselves and to appreciate the joy of its meaning. All that a child learns about love, about security, about right and wrong, about forgiveness, and about his own worth and dignity, he is likely to learn first from his parents. If a child is to learn about the love that God has for him because he is God's child, it will be primarily from his parents that he will learn it. They love him for his own sake, not because he is good or obedient or beautiful, but because he is their child.

God is using the earthly parents as the agents of his love for his children, asking them to guard them and love them and care for them and lead them for his sake. They are partners with God as much as with one another in the adventure of home-building. If they manage to make this explicit as well as implicit, any children will more easily be led to discover its meaning for themselves. For instance, the simple practice of saying grace at meals is one of the easiest ways of expressing this partnership; the parents have worked to earn enough to buy the food (produced with the aid of men's labours), but the ultimate truth remains that all things are the gift of God. To say (or sing), 'Be present at our table, Lord' will not make him any more present (for he is there already and always), but it can make his presence more real to us.

Then the bond of love within the home has significance for society. If God is love and if the secret of eternal life is that men should know God and find him in Christ, then anything which lets that love be seen on earth is of ultimate importance. If the partners to a marriage are bound together with a love which comes from God, that is to say a love which is 'out of this world', then their home will reveal this to the world. There are so many meanings to the word 'love' in English, and too often the world looks at love the wrong way. Romance is too often associated with infatuation, being 'swept off your feet'. In a sense this is good, for love takes you further than cold reason is prepared to go. Again, the world is often accused of being too concerned about the sexual expression of love; in fact, the world sees only half the beauty and wonder of sex. The bond of unconditional love and trust and loyalty places physical love in a new context. Every good bridegroom thinks his bride is the most beautiful girl in the world. As an outward and tangible expression of a love which is exclusive, freely given, and lasting, the sexual side of our nature takes on a new dignity and is enriched beyond words. When earthly love is ennobled in this way, a home becomes secure because it is held together by love which is unqualified and unconditional, and society is presented with a challenge and also ground for encouragement. The distinctive quality of such a home stands as a witness that this is what married life should be and can be.

But the giving and keeping of a pledge of unqualified and unconditional love enables the partners in a marriage themselves to discern in that love something which is of God — for this is the kind of love which God has for us, and which he has shown in Jesus. For better or worse, in prosperity or trouble, in sickness or in health, he loves us without limit, for there are no limits to his love. There are no limits to its embrace; all are equally the objects of his love. There are also no limits to its extent; the cross is the permanent assurance that nothing on earth, however evil, can quench the love of God. In a marriage where the bond is of this quality, the love of God is seen to break through on to the canvas of space and time. It is difficult to believe in this kind of love. It is easier to imagine that God loves good people more than bad people, sensible people more than foolish ones, and kind people more than cruel ones. But God loves them all equally and without limit. When a partner in a marriage discovers that he is loved like that, when he discovers he is forgiven and knows that he does not deserve it but that love is being freely and willingly given, then he has seen something of God.

Christian marriage is not only a gateway to love, but also to faith and hope. The promises made at a wedding are not just expressions of love, but declarations of faith; for faith is a readiness to go into the unknown. In a marriage, each declares a readiness to go through life with the other, come what may. What the future holds, neither knows. While prudence and foresight are sensible, too great an anxiety for security takes away from the joy which comes from mutual trust in facing a future which is unknown. Indeed, this mutual trust is based on very limited knowledge of each other, for at the time of marriage that knowledge is certainly limited. Neither knows all about the other; nor would it be right to expect (or try to demand) knowledge which is not freely given. But this very fact is a help to the understanding of faith, for there is all the difference between believing things about a person and believing in that person. One does not get married because on the strength of information received, one believes the other has certain desirable qualities. On the contrary, each desires to know the other better, and is so moved by the little he does know of the other that he is prepared to go through life with the other. Each accepts the promise of the other at its face value and discovers the richness of its value later. Faith in God is very much like that also. We do not know all about him, and Christians may even disagree about some of the things they think they do know. But they are prepared to accept him as Lord and Guide and Master, and to go through life with him. Perhaps there is some symbolism in the fact that at a wedding the partners arrive at the Chancel step independently and then walk together to the Communion rail where they kneel, there to discover that Christ is with them in their walk through life.

With faith and love there is also hope. If faith is a readiness to face the unknown, hope is the confidence that things will be for the best. Love always looks for the best, and hope always expects the best, in others. It is natural and right that parents are full of hope for their children. In relation to God, hope is the confidence that all things work together for good to them that love him. Thus, hope is not blind, but rather the fruit of love given freely; it is because we know we are loved that the future becomes filled with hope.

This kind of faith and love and hope take us out of the realm of justice and merit into the realm of mercy and generosity. Each loves the other for his or her own sake and seeks the good of the other at any cost to self. Each learns from the freely-given love of the other something of the love of God. It is also possible for the parents of either partner to see something new in the love of God when son or daughter comes to be married. Almost of necessity there is something possessive, even selfish, in parental love; for in the earliest years they have had complete responsibility for their child. They give their child food and protection, love and guidance, precept and example, security and forgiveness. Naturally, they want the very best for their own child, and when they see possible danger (to body, mind, or soul) they do what they can to prevent the danger developing into damage. Out of their love for their child and their desire that no hurt should come his way comes the resistance to the giving of the greatest gift of all — that of freedom. Freedom ultimately includes freedom to make mistakes, freedom to reject accepted standards, freedom to give hurt, unknowingly or even consciously, and it is this even more than jealousy which makes it costly for parents to give their children the precious gift of freedom. Yet in the Marriage Service this is expressed in an act the significance of which has changed with the change in the status of woman, namely the act of 'giving away the bride'. There are, of course, societies in which daughters are still regarded as possessions, but even in modern western society the courtesy of asking the girl's father before announcing an engagement has by no means died. In the Marriage Service, the minister still asks who gives the bride to be married and the father (or friend) takes the hand of his daughter and passes it into the hand of the priest. In doing this, he acknowledges that the responsibility for his daughter laid upon him by God is now fulfilled by his recognition of her freedom to marry. A new non-possessive relationship begins between parent and child which has a rich quality all of its own.

In the Marriage Service, the phrase is used that in marriage 'there is signified and represented the spiritual marriage and unity between Christ and his Church'. The unity of the one with the other expressed in the description of the Church as the Body of Christ, and the distinctness of the one from the other expressed in the description of the Church

c

as the Bride of Christ give us some glimpse of the meaning of this phrase. The conjunction of the words 'love and honour' in the marriage vow reveals the same thought; for love seeks more and more unity with the other, and honour respects the individuality, indeed the very 'other-ness' of the other. By entering into an understanding of these aspects of the marriage bond, one is given some glimpse of the relation between Christ and ourselves. He became man, and as man he lived and died to redeem us; yet as our divine saviour and risen Lord we accord him our worship.

It is not in the least to be expected that any of these thoughts are in the mind of the couple when they arrive at the church for their wedding. They are at the beginning of an adventure, and hopefully they are aware that it has more than just an earthly dimension. But by the grace of God they will discover, in the richness and depth of their relationship, something which leads them beyond the visible and tangible to a glimpse of the love of the eternal God.

4

GOD'S STRENGTH IN WEAKNESS

What has the Christian faith to say about sickness, and what does God, made known in Christ, offer to man in his sickness? If all sickness were primarily physical (like a broken leg or toothache), the task of understanding it would be fairly easy, especially when the prospects of the patient returning to full health are good. Much sickness is hard to fit into the general pattern of the created order and difficult to reconcile with a belief that this world is the scene of activity of a loving and all-powerful God. In some cases, our sickness may result from our own fault; being sorry for ourselves will not make us better. In some cases, sickness may result from the fault of another; being cross about it will not make us better. Understanding why a person is ill may be very satisfying to the inquisitive intellect but does little to promote the work of healing.

I suppose it is natural to try to see how sickness can be explained, but the theory that sickness is God's punishment for human sin is hard to maintain. Those who brought to Jesus the man who had been blind from birth certainly held this view (John 9.1-7). Since the man had been born blind, it was hard to see how it could have been because of his own sin; perhaps it was the consequence of some sin of his father and that this was being visited upon his child — that would be perfectly possible, for promiscuity on the part of parents can result in venereal disease for themselves and a variety of handicaps for their children. But Jesus turns their question aside. God was not punishing this man for his own or his father's sin; God's concern was the healing of the blind man, and in that healing men would see the activity of God if they themselves had eyes to see. The fact that some did not recognize the healing as an act of God merely revealed their own blindness (John 9.39-41).

It is one thing to say that sickness is not sent by God as a punishment for sin (though occasionally it may be the consequence of sin), but this does not mean that sickness is part of God's will for his children. The fact that God allows sickness and pain does not mean that he wishes it to be. Healing is his will and, when it happens, healing is his action. On the other hand, it is not possible to divide body and soul and to say that sickness belongs to the body and is the concern of the medical profession while sin belongs to the soul and is the concern of the Church. There is an element of truth in this, but it is far from being the whole truth. Neither body nor soul is the whole man; each affects the other. Doctors know that many physical disorders have their origin in mental or spiritual strain; equally, a physical disorder can easily prove to be partly the cause of bad temper or cowardice or pride. Body, mind, and spirit together make up the whole man; it is difficult, if not impossible, to draw the boundary lines as though they were ingredients in a recipe. Man is a unity. Healing and wholeness of body, mind, and spirit belong together. It is not surprising that sickness and sin are commonly linked, nor that the sin must be cured before there can be complete healing of body. In contrast with those who brought the blind man to Jesus, those who brought the paralytic were expecting a physical healing and no more. When Jesus declared that the man's sins were forgiven, they were offended (Matt. 9.2-8; Mark 2.1-12). Whether this particular person was paralysed as a consequence of sin, we cannot now know; the story illustrates the unity of physical and spiritual in the mind of Jesus. An equally vivid illustration is that of the man who lay by the Pool of Bethesda. He was sorry for himself, and the fact that he had been there for thirty-eight years suggests that he 'enjoyed bad health'; he looked for sympathy rather than healing (John 5.1-9). Indeed, the form of the question put by Jesus, 'Do you want to be made well again?', goes to the heart of his problem; his mind and his will combined to prevent any healing taking place.

Man is a unity. Surgeon, physician, psychiatrist, and priest are helping to bring wholeness to people who are sick, not separately to bodies, minds, and spirits. The will to be well again affects the whole process of healing. This may be more obvious, perhaps, in behavioural diseases like alcoholism than in the mending of a broken leg or the last stages of lung cancer. It is understandable that we find in the Gospels that Jesus often said to the sick, 'Thy faith hath made thee whole.' A most valuable role is played by those who visit the sick when they strengthen the will to live and provide the incentive; indeed, sometimes it is necessary to go beyond pointing to the value of life and to point to the duty to try to live (for the sake of wife, or husband, or children). Often it needs to be said plainly that it matters to other people that one should be healed. It matters to God.

Not only is a man a combination of body, mind, and spirit, which cannot be separated, but also no person is complete in himself. A man who is wrapped up in himself is without love, which is the essence of real, or eternal, life; he only needs physical death to complete the process of isolation from life of any kind. In biblical language, 'We are members one of another' (Eph. 4.25). This has an important bearing on the whole question, for an individual cannot be made whole as an isolated unit. Primarily at the physical level, the medical profession is bringing the resources of mankind's knowledge and skill and nursing attention to bear on the patient's condition. The physician or surgeon is part of a large team, and his actions are the expression of the desire of very many others that the patient should recover. Primarily at the spiritual level, the pastoral care of the parish priest and the prayers of the Church (and the patient's friends) are bringing the resources of the love and concern of others to bear on the patient's condition. Both are agents of Christ, through whom God's healing power is conveyed. Sometimes the hands of the priest may be laid on the patient with prayer, to focus the strengthening power of God and the support of the Body of Christ. The isolation of the patient in either case is being broken down, and so the process of healing made easier.

Even the practice of making a special confession of sin in a time of sickness can have a healing effect. The act of confession and declaration of forgiveness assures the patient that the barriers between himself and God, and between himself and others, caused by his own

sin are thrown down. To be forgiven is to be in
fellowship with God and man (1 John 1.5-7), and this
obviously is the right reason for making a confession
of our sin; the healing effect is an earthly by-product,
but none the less real for that. Similarly, laying on
hands with prayer and the anointing of the sick with
oil, a practice referred to in Scripture (1 Jas. 5.14-15),
is no form of magic, any more than Communion of
the sick is some form of divine medicine. Especially
when the priest brings bread and wine which have
been consecrated at a Communion Service shared by
others in church, the Communion acts as a strong
link between the patient and the rest of the Body of
Christ; sharing the one bread, their membership of
the one Body is made more real. Further, since the
common life of the Body is the life of Christ himself,
the action of the patient in Communion is a means
of allowing the life of Christ to be linked with his
own life; this is in itself an act of healing.

Spiritual care for the sick does not all consist of
raising the will to live, ministering Communion, and
laying on hands, nor does it all take place when there
is actual visiting. The faith and the prayers of others,
known or unknown to the sick person, are accepted
and used by God as instruments of healing. Similarly,
while Jesus often commented on the faith of the sick
person, in several instances it is the faith of a third
party which is accepted as a means of healing (Matt. 9.
2-8; 8.10; 15.28, for example), when there is no
indication that the sick person had shown any sign of
faith. One of the most vivid examples of this is the
story of the centurion whose son was at the point of
death (John 4.46-53). His father, hearing that Jesus

C2

was not too far away, left his dying son in the hope that he might fetch Jesus just in time. That in itself was an act of faith. To be asked to return on his own, after taking a whole day to find the Healer, having only been told by him that his son would live, was an even greater test of his faith. (Add to this that it was a Roman, an officer of the occupying power, who was going all that way to bring a Jew to his home, and the test of faith is seen even more clearly.) It is clear from the story in the Gospel that the father's faith was taken and used for the healing of his son.

This still holds good. Instances of the faith and prayers of believers being taken and used by God for the healing of others are fortunately frequent, though none the less marvellous for their frequency. Such faith and prayer will be costly; far more is needed than the casual mention of a name in a prayer for the sick in general. Our faith may be tested by the sincerity and intensity of our prayer. It is not that God will forget, or be unwilling to help unless we continually remind him, that we are told to pray without ceasing; constant prayer on our part is a measure of the extent of our concern and of our faith in the promise of Jesus that 'What things soever ye desire, when ye pray, believe that ye receive them and ye shall have them' (Mark 11.24). If we believe our prayer will be answered, we can picture our sick friend in his need; we can picture the risen Christ coming to him and standing by him. His divine strength meets his human weakness, giving confidence and allaying fear. We make our prayer that the deepest and most genuine needs of our friend may be met. How God uses the faith and prayers of others to help those in need is indeed a mystery, but that he does so is the experience of many and a cause for great thanksgiving.

While most people would hesitate to describe any particular sickness as God's visitation, times of sickness can certainly be used as occasions of growth in faith and prayer. Those who are self-reliant find in times of sickness that they are now dependent on others; those who plan their own lives (and those of others) a long time ahead now find that they have to live one day at a time. God gives us grace and power and guidance, day by day. In sickness, the physical and spiritual expressions of this combine. Medicine, exercise, food, and endurance must be accepted one day at a time; yesterday's supply does not serve today's need. The Lord's Prayer reminds us of this same truth, for Jesus taught us to pray, 'Give us *this day* our daily bread.' The sick person who really grasps this truth is likely to shame some of us who are well by his cheerfulness. He has learned not to worry but to trust, which is one of the most basic lessons of the Sermon on the Mount. If a spell of sickness is the occasion of learning that lesson, then we may rightly thank God for it even if he did not send it for that purpose. The Psalmist said, 'It is good for me that I have been in trouble, that I might learn thy judgements' (Ps. 119.71).

Then again, there can be a fellowship of suffering between those who are ill which can be the means of breaking down the barriers between themselves and others, and between themselves and Christ. This fellowship shows itself in a light-hearted way often in an orthopaedic ward where apparently serious men behave like schoolboys with their plaster casts and artificial limbs. But at all levels, sickness attacks self-sufficiency and makes fellowship with others in a similar plight easier. In a time of common misfortune, as in wartime, those who shared danger and hardship found themselves in the same situation as many others, and the hardships were correspondingly lightened. This sharing of misfortune with others can be a first step towards understanding that Christ shared human life and human suffering. The secret of the Christian faith is that he shared our life and makes it possible for us to share his life. Our weakness and his strength can come together. The life that he invites us to share is not only stronger than sickness, it is stronger than death.

He shared his strength during his earthly ministry. When the woman with the issue of blood reached out to touch him, Jesus asked, 'Who touched me?' When the bystanders pointed to the size of the crowd, Jesus persisted that someone had touched him, for he had perceived that strength had gone out of him (Luke 8. 43-8). This is not an unknown or even an uncommon experience. In a variety of ways, sitting with the sick and listening to the troubles of others 'takes it out of you'. This is not because of conscious effort, for one often seems to be doing nothing but sit and watch and listen; but patient listening can be hard work, and it is not meaningless when a person who has talked to you for half an hour then thanks you for all the help you have given him when in fact you have not said a word. If there can be a sharing of human weakness and strength, of human anxiety and confident calm, how much more can there be a sharing of our weakness and Christ's divine strength.

> I am weak, but thou art mighty;
> Hold me with thy powerful hand.

A particular example of this is at the time of death. The dying seem to have a way of knowing when those whom they love and who love them are with them. You do not stop them from dying just by being there, though a last-minute rally (of recognition and gratitude?) is by no means uncommon. They do not want good advice or a long explanation of what it means to die; they want you. You take their hand, you speak to reassure them; your calmness and strength support them in their frailty. If this happens because you are there, how much more if they are aware of the presence of the risen Christ. He shared human death, and he is risen and alive for ever; he invites us to share his life, and in doing so the Christian can face death with quiet confidence and without fear, for he does it in Christ's strength instead of his own weakness.

5

THE SIN OF MAN AND THE LOVE OF GOD

Sunday by Sunday, at any of the regular services of the Church, we are all invited to join in a general Confession of some sort and, whether we have prepared ourselves or not, we join in. Central among the symbols of the Christian faith is the cross, and central to the teaching of the Christian faith is some statement to the effect that Christ died for our sins. Now most of us are not criminals or notorious sinners in the sense that other people turn their backs on us because of the kind of people we are. Most of us are fairly kind, respectable people. It may be a judgement on us as Christians, but we probably accept and welcome one another not so much because we are fellow-Christians as because we have roughly similar outlooks and generally respect each other. This is not wholly surprising nor wholly regrettable. Church-going people are likely to have had the sort of upbringing that would make them law-abiding citizens; they are likely to have the sort of background that would keep them what they have become. Their temptations and their besetting sins may be different from those of the unbeliever, and the spiritual dangers of respectability are no less serious on that account.

When we do not respect a person, we probably try to avoid his company. When we read in a newspaper of people who batter babies or steal from pensioners or traffic in drugs or indulge in various forms of

44

violence, we probably hope we shall not get involved
with them. But if one of these people happened to be a
member of our own family, it would be quite different.
So long as we are not personally involved, we can read
about these people and think about them without
much emotion. For instance, we can coolly read the
story of Delilah, the prostitute who was paid by the
Philistines to catch out Samson and discover his secret.
Newspapers of today are likely to bear record of the
exploits of similar political call-girls. But how do their
relatives, their parents, and their friends feel? They
cannot just read the story without feeling, and then
pass on to read the financial or the sports reports.
Where love is involved, the whole situation is altered.

Parents have their own ideals as to the kind of boy
or girl they hope their son or daughter will grow up to
become. By precept and by example, they try to set
certain standards for their children. If they are wise,
they want their children to recognize for themselves
the rightness of the standards they set and to live up
to those standards of their own will. For this to happen, they must be given freedom which is not true
freedom unless it includes the power to disobey, the
freedom to go one's own way. Freedom in the last
resort includes the right to say 'No': though the
society in which this happens has the right to protect
itself from some of the consequences of that refusal.
In an imperfect world, we have to seek a halfway house
between that complete anarchy which would result
from a society having no standards or rules or rulers
and a society without real freedom, when the word of
the dictator is obeyed without question even if not
without fear. But the relationships of a family are

different from those of a club, a team, a company, or a nation. In a team, for example, a person who refuses to play as a co-operative member can be dropped; the person who will not obey the law of the land stands the risk of going to prison. A family is different. It is not held together by rules and punishments. In those cases where rejection does take place, there is recognition of failure not only on the part of the member rejected but on the part of the family who reject him. In a very real sense it can be said that the family itself has broken up. It is basic to the teaching of Jesus that God wants the human race to be a family, to address him as Father, with all the understanding and love that should accompany that attitude.

God gives men freedom, including the freedom not to do his will. To say this implies that we can know his will, even if imperfectly, and it is part of our Christian faith that God does reveal his will. Central to the teaching of the Old Testament is the declaring of the law and word of God. This word is declared both in general, as in the Ten Commandments, and also in particular through the words of a prophet to an individual. Often the mode of communication is left completely vague, and it is merely said, 'The Lord said to So-and-so'. Man's conscience is one instrument which God uses to prompt to action, or to restrain. The picture-language of the story of Jonah rings true to human experience. He was told to go and do one thing and he promptly said to himself, 'I'm not doing that; I am going my own way'; immediately, having been told to go to Nineveh, he went down and took a ship somewhere else. He knew perfectly well what he was doing; he was running away from his duty, from his responsibility.

Awareness of responsibility and the ability to say 'No' constitute the basis of the moral freedom given by God to man. The method by which we become aware of duty or responsibility may take many different forms, from the written word to the spoken word of another (who may not always be conscious of the significance of his words), from the dictates of public morality to the promptings of private conscience. The nature of the duty may not be precise, nor our interpretation of it necessarily exact. But none of these things takes away from the basic principle that man has a sense that there are things he ought to do, and that this responsibility is laid on him not only by his duty to his neighbour. The nature of man's disobedience also varies, from direct refusal to an attempt (like Pilate) to wash our hands of all responsibility, from deliberate self-deception regarding the issue involved to a progressive deafness of conscience.

There are those who are so wrapped up in their own concerns that they just don't think. How many times have children excused themselves by saying, 'I didn't think.' That was the whole trouble — they didn't think, and they ought to have thought. If we do not think, we do not know what we have left undone; it makes saying the general Confession much easier! There are those who are so wrapped up in their own concerns that their sense of duty is too limited. The priest and the Levite in the parable of the Good Samaritan may have had plenty of reasons for not stopping to help, including the fact that they were on their way to do something else. Excuses are ready to hand when we are engaged in one task and it would put us out to direct our attention to another.

Then there are those who set their own judgement about what is right and wrong against that of the Bible or the Church or, indeed, any other outside authority. They say that things have changed since the days the Scriptures were written, that social conditions have changed, and that we must not be bound by the conventions of the past. Each person, they would say, must judge for himself what is right or wrong for him. There is certainly an element of truth in this. Conscience must always be followed; equally important, conscience must be informed. Some of the detailed instructions of the Old Testament may not apply in our changed society. The spotlight on human character which the Old Testament provides reveals some weaknesses which we see today. Intrigue, jealousy and greed, dishonesty and pride (which includes forgetfulness of God), disloyalty and failure to keep one's word, cruelty and the desire for revenge, are not the private property of any one age, ancient or modern. The more one reads the Old Testament, let alone the New Testament, the plainer it appears that human nature has not changed much over the centuries and that the underlying motives of men are the same now as then; the basic elements of right and wrong have not changed, and the task of man is not to decide but to discover the moral law.

Again, it is no new complaint that dishonest and greedy and proud people often seem to prosper and to be unaware of anything wrong with themselves or of the suffering to others that their way of life causes. This world is not so organized that the wicked and selfish suffer while the kind and unselfish prosper.

In a world of limited resources, if one man or one group or one nation is selfish and greedy, someone else will go hungry; sooner or later when the cause of injustice is recognized, he will be angry and want to get his own back. The simple analysis given in the Epistle of St James (Jas. 4. 1-2), that wars and fighting are the consequence of inner conflicts, remains true. The human desire to get level, partly out of a sense of justice and partly out of a sense of revenge, is very strong in individuals and equally strong in nations and groups. Much of it arises from the fact that almost any sin causes someone else to suffer or be hurt, materially or mentally or spiritually. Cruelty causes pain, and matrimonial disloyalty causes jealousy and anger quite apart from the untold suffering as a result of the insecurity caused to any children. A proud person arouses the scorn of others, the greedy and the selfish cause others to be in want. Perhaps the supreme sin is being so selfish that we do not care, but become wholly unmindful and unaware of the consequence of our way of life on the lives of others. The casual phrase, 'I couldn't care less', sums up the extreme of human self-centredness.

It is of the essence of the Christian gospel that God couldn't care more (for all people and for all time) and that his caring has been shown uniquely, once and for all, in the cross of Christ. Attempts to explain the meaning of the cross, theories of the atonement as they are called, vary widely, and some of the imagery used (not least the biblical imagery of ransom) does not always strike a note of response today. It is one thing to say that Jesus died for our sins or to sing, 'He died that we might be forgiven', but each

D

generation needs to seek to understand this fact and interpret it afresh in its own thought-form. As each generation does this, some new vision is given to the many-sided richness of the love and mercy of God. The old interpretations are not discarded or denied, but rather enriched by being seen in a new light. So it is that today the categories of rejection and acceptance may be more meaningful than those which brought home to people of earlier times the meaning of the cross.

Rejection takes many forms. Sometimes no attempt is made to justify it and the action is instinctive rather than deliberate. A driver is going a long journey in his car and passes hitch-hikers without any serious thought; if he did think, he might well try to justify his action and he might make out quite a good case for himself. His action in going past without stopping is his way of saying, 'I don't want to be involved with you.' Turning away the hawker, canvasser, or beggar who comes to our door is a similar but more conscious act. Small children can be quite devastating in their rejection of other children, and the bitterness caused can go very deep; the reasons may be trivial, such as not being clean or having been born with some disfigurement, but the hurt is anything but trivial. On an adult level, anyone with a pet theory or a favourite good cause is liable to be brushed aside by those who do not want to be distracted. Idealists who serve on committees, or Parochial Church Councils, to say nothing of Synods, are in great danger of constant rejection; the other members have not the time to be bothered with them. This rejection is easily 'justified' on the grounds that they can be guaranteed to have their say next time, whatever happens.

These examples may seem very slight instances of rejection, and one could quote far more serious examples. The trade-unionist who believes an agreed industrial action by his union to be wrong lays himself open to rejection if he defies his union. The pacifist who refuses to fight for his country understandably lays himself open to similar action. The vast number of abortions now performed annually in this country provides more examples of rejection; each is an example of saying to the unborn child, 'I don't want you.' The equally vast number of divorces, whatever their cause, is a similar example. Children rejected by their parents, and parents rejected by their children; immigrants shunned by their white neighbours; ex-prisoners on the one hand and do-gooders on the other are avoided because to accept them would disturb one's way of living. The list could be endless.

The cross can be seen clearly in this light. For a variety of quite different reasons, people were saying, 'We don't want this man, Jesus.' The Jewish religious leaders did not want him because he challenged their authority; he set himself up to speak in the name of God, claiming an authority equal to the Scriptures of which they were the guardians and interpreters. 'Ye have heard that it hath been said . . . but I say unto you . . . ' The challenge reached a climax in the cleansing of the Temple (if the order of events in the first three Gospels is followed), but the ultimate conflict was that of the source of authority, and the religious leaders could not accept his claims. When challenged on oath to say whether he was the Christ, Jesus continued his claims, and the High Priest understandably considered the case proved against Jesus (Matt. 26.63-6; Mark 14.61-3).

Pontius Pilate, the local embodiment of Roman power, had the responsibility of maintaining law and order. If Jesus had incited the Jews to rebellion, or had gone round teaching that it was unlawful to pay tribute to Caesar, the task of Pontius Pilate would have been simple. As far as he was concerned, it was the Jews who wanted to be rid of Jesus. It was a Jewish problem. When, however, he was afraid of a Jewish uprising he was prepared to sign the death warrant for the sake of peace. His rejection of Jesus was of a very different kind from that of the Jews, and he tried to wash his hands of responsibility, but he put his signature to the demand, 'Let him be crucified.'

For precisely the opposite reason, the Zealot party were glad to be rid of Jesus. He spoke of freedom but did not use violent means to achieve it for the Jewish people. The age of freedom fighters is not new. When the Zealots, whose hearts were set on the liberation of the Jews, looked at Jesus they were prepared to cry, 'Give us Barabbas rather than him.' The list could be extended greatly. Peter denied him to save his own skin. Judas had handed him over to the Jewish leaders for reasons not made clear. The traders and money-changers in the Temple would undoubtedly have rejoiced to see him go. But the crucifixion could not have taken place had it not been for the willingness of the crowd, who a few days before had shouted, 'Hosanna to the Son of David.' That crowd, at the instigation of the Jewish rulers, were now ready to shout, 'We have no King but Caesar. Crucify him.'

Uninformed and easily led, they were the victims of propaganda; modern parallels are not hard to find. Without the support of the popular vote, there would not have been a crucifixion.

All these people and many others were bound up in the whole process which led up to the crucifixion. It is clear from the Scriptures that some were involved through weakness against their will and better judgement, Simon Peter and Pontius Pilate in particular. In the story of the crucifixion we see jealousy, spite, prejudice, treachery and cowardice, gullible weak-will, pride and hatred, focused at one point. It was as though the whole of mankind were saying to the incarnate Son of God, 'We don't want you.' Jesus, without violence or resistance or retaliation, accepted all the evil that man could do to him, and it led him to the cross. The cross, in this sense, is the revelation of the evil of man; it is a showing forth of the wickedness of sin. There was throughout the life of Jesus this struggle between the love of God and the evil of man, and the struggle went on to the very cross. It was a real struggle and one side or the other had to break. The evil of man nailed Christ to the cross. It was the greatest sin that man has ever committed, but this did not break or alter the love of God — 'Father, forgive them' is Christ's prayer at the moment of the climax of human sin. Christians believe that that prayer has been and is still answered. There is no limit to the love of God. When man says to God, 'I do not want you, and I want to live my life without you,' God says back, 'But I love you; I want you to be able to live with me for ever.'

This takes us to the heart of the meaning of

forgiveness which is a matter of personal relationship
between God and man, and not a ledger transaction
in which so much sin is cancelled by so much
suffering. The cross is a demonstration of the love of
God in spite of the sin of man. Indeed, it is more than
a demonstration, for God's love was not only revealed
but tested. If on the one hand we cannot earn the
good will of God by good works, no more can we lose
it by our sin. God loves us, with an infinite love, just
as we are. This is good news; this is gospel. What we
have to do is so to respond that we make our own
that which God has done for us in Christ.

God's love for man did not change on Good Friday;
that love has always been infinite. Man's knowledge
of that love, however, was changed entirely on Good
Friday. Men can now know, and not just hope, that
they can be forgiven. To have that knowledge we have
to turn to Christ, for if we want to bring our sins to
be taken away by the love of God we must turn to that
event when in time and space man's sin and God's
love are seen to come together in focus. We look first
at Christ to see the meaning of divine love, and not
first at ourselves to see the depth of our sin. Indeed,
we shall never realize the depth of our sin until we
see the extent of his love. It is only 'When I survey
the wondrous cross on which the Prince of Glory
died' that I can turn to myself and 'pour contempt on
all my pride'. Looking unto Jesus is the start of our
faith, as it will be the fulness of our joy when faith
is turned into sight.

We look first then at Jesus crucified because of
man's sin, and as a consequence we look at ourselves,
our pride, our neglect of our neighbour (often

largely unconscious, though no less culpable), our selfishness and weak will, our jealousy and cowardice. These contributed to bring Jesus to the cross. None of us would like the whole of our lives, all our thoughts and actions and motives past and present, displayed on a 23-inch screen for everyone to see. We should be ashamed to meet what we thought were our friends. If we think we wouldn't mind, we are bluffing. 'If we say that we have no sins, we deceive ourselves and the truth is not in us' (1 John 1.8). If we look at ourselves first, before looking at the cross, this may happen. But if we look at the cross first, and then turn to look at ourselves and see our sin in its light, then we can turn to Christ and say, 'I am sorry, not for my sake because of the state I am in. I now begin to realize what my sin means to you, and I am sorry for your sake.' Real penitence is not just regretting what we have done; most of us often regret what we have done for all sorts of reasons which have nothing to do with penitence. Real penitence begins when we see what our sin means to God, and we are sorry for that reason. We see this in the cross, which has made it possible for man to be penitent and as a result to be forgiven.

There was one condition that Jesus laid down, if we could expect to be forgiven. It was that we should ourselves forgive others. The petition in the Lord's Prayer is plain, 'Forgive us . . . as we forgive.' We find this point made repeatedly in our Lord's teaching. We are to love others, as he has loved us. We are to be merciful, as our Father in heaven is merciful. If God loves us in spite of what we have done and, as a consequence, have become (and he does) then we must love others in spite of what they may do to us. This is the demand of God upon us; he also gives us the grace which goes with it. As we become sensitive to our own sin, so we become a little more understanding, a little more humble and sensitive to the weakness of others. This is indeed a very gracious gift of God.

There are times when our minds may tell us that it is true that we are forgiven, but our hearts are still in need of assurance. We should like to hear it said by Christ himself. 'Do not be afraid. It really is true that I love you, accept you, and can use you, just as you are.' There is a ministry in the Church to help us when we need to hear just that. Every priest at his ordination is commissioned to be the spokesman of Christ, especially in the matter of the declaration of God's forgiveness of sin. Any churchman may go to his vicar, or to any other priest, and ask for opportunity to make a confession of sin. The priest may not at any time tell any other person (nor even remind the penitent) anything of what he has heard in such a private confession. If it is a domestic matter, he may not tell husband or wife, parent or child; whatever is said is said to God in the presence of a priest rather than to the priest himself. When he pronounces absolution, it is God's forgiveness which he is declaring. There is, however, a further significance in this ministry. Our sins not only are a grief to God, the measure of that grief being shown in the cross; they also wound the Body of Christ on earth now. By our sins we weaken the witness of the Body of Christ and others who do not belong to the Body are hindered from loving Christ. The witness of our fellow Christians within the Church, which is the Body of Christ, is to some extent frustrated by our sin. We need, therefore, not only to be assured of the forgiveness of God but also to be reconciled to the Church. The priest is acting as the spokesman of the Body of Christ, the Church, when he declares God's forgiveness. By his declaration that we are absolved of our sins, he is also declaring that the Church accepts us just as we are. This means that when we next come to Holy Communion, with our fellow Christians in the one Body, we can draw near with faith and confidence and receive the sacrament to our comfort.

6

DEATH AND LIFE

What happens after we die? The question has fascinated men all down the ages, and the burial customs discovered from excavating tombs all over the world witness to the variety of human hopes and beliefs. *In memoriam* notices in local newspapers witness to a remarkable variety of opinions in our own day! The imagery commonly used includes such phrases as passed over, passed on, entered into life through the gate of death, departed this life, and others of the same sort. Death is one of the puzzles of this world. There is a sense in which we feel it ought not to happen, since life is so real and the awareness of being alive is so real also. It is hard, if not impossible, to imagine that there could be a time when we shall no longer be alive. Yet, though we cannot imagine the state of not being alive, we know that death will come to us. Death is real, and we all share in it irrespective of colour, creed, or moral worth. We all share the same human nature, and that human nature includes the death of the body. In Adam, all die.

Sometimes death comes after a long, full, and happy life as a gentle release from possible suffering. This is by no means what always happens; the parson's task would be much easier if it were. Death may come to a person of any age, including small children; it may come as the consequence of illness, or as the result of an accident, or as the consequence of war. In wartime we were all more conscious of the uncertainty of life. 'In the midst of life we are in death' is true enough; yet in so many cases, death seems so unreasonable.

One reaction to this is to shrug one's shoulders and say, 'Let us eat, drink, and be merry, for tomorrow we die.' The writer of the Wisdom of Solomon (2.1-9) describes the same problem of the shortness and uncertainty of life, and goes on to describe the consequent action of the ungodly in pursuing their own selfish aims irrespective of their effect on others. He then concludes, 'As for the mysteries of God, they knew them not; neither hoped they for the wages of righteousness nor discerned a reward for blameless souls. For God created man to be immortal, and made him to be an image of his own eternity' (2.22-4). He also faces the question of untimely death, first by saying, 'Honourable age is not that which standeth in length of time, nor that is measured by number of years. But wisdom is the grey hair unto men and an unspotted life is old age. He pleased God and was beloved of Him; so that living among sinners, he was translated. Yea, speedily was he taken away, lest that wickedness should alter his understanding or deceit beguile his soul . . . . For his soul pleased the Lord; therefore hasted he to take him away from among the wicked' (4.8-14). All this is in the context of the affirmation, 'The souls of the righteous are in the hand of God, and there shall no torment touch them' (3.1).

This is about as far as one can go without the knowledge of Christ. Man is meant to be immortal. There is nothing to prove it, and it is a hope that arises from the paradox of death. Life is unreasonable if it all comes to an end with the death of the body, as though we had risen for a moment above the waters of consciousness, and found love and friendship, pursued ideals of human dignity, grasped some truths which we thought to be timeless, felt some awareness of a God whom we believed to be eternal, and then sunk back again into eternal oblivion. The hope of immortality is our protest against the unreasonableness of death.

But is this not all wishful thinking? If one person cares to think that there is nothing to look forward to after death, and another person cares to think that there is, is there any reason why either should change his opinion? Unless there is some evidence, each can think what he likes. Here, precisely, is the point. The Christian claim is that there is some evidence which gives ground for belief that there is a life to look forward to after death. In the Gospel records, we have stories of the resurrection of Jesus after he had been seen by many people to have died. These stories enshrine one of the central facts of the Christian faith. Critics have pointed out every conceivable difficulty. The stories are not easy to grasp. Two men walk with the risen Jesus for some two hours, talking with him, but do not recognize him until he breaks bread in their home; he then vanishes from their sight (Luke 24.30-1). Twice he comes to the disciples in an upper room, the doors being shut for fear of the Jews; yet on one of these occasions, he invites Thomas to see and handle the wounds in his body (John 20.27). On another occasion, when the disciples are wondering whether what they are seeing is a ghost, he eats in their presence and claims that ghosts do not have flesh and bones, and he has (Luke 24.36-43). Yet the stories are there, written after the Church had been proclaiming the risen Christ as Lord for many years, and one cannot ignore them. Whether one believes in the resurrection of Jesus Christ or not, the manuscript evidence in its support is more extensive than for any other event prior to the invention of printing. Nor can one escape from the evidence of human nature. Something overwhelming must have happened to turn a group of frightened followers, the leader of whom saved his skin by telling a slave girl he had never heard of Jesus, into a band of men who preached the resurrection of Jesus to the very people who had put him to death. This they did at the risk, and in many cases the cost, of their lives. There must be something to account for the gallant deaths of the martyrs, who would not deny their faith in Christ's resurrection. There must be something to account for the holy and happy death of countless believers, who looked beyond the hurdle of death to a life shared with the risen Christ. Any experienced priest is likely to have witnessed many such deaths.

All this does not amount to proof. We live by faith and not by logical proof. The stories of the resurrection, however, do enshrine one of the central tenets of the Christian faith which is proclaimed alike by Christians of all traditions. Christians may be divided about many other things, they are divided about very many matters of Church order and of ethics. About the gospel of the resurrection they are agreed. Christ is risen from the dead; Jesus lives. It does not follow that every Christian starts by believing the stories and then comes to accept their consequence (that Christ is alive now), and afterwards comes to some experience which he interprets as an awareness of, or even an encounter with, the living Christ. There are indeed Christians who find the resurrection stories credible because they have had an experience which is inexplicable unless it is true that Christ is alive; such Christians are met by Christ as truly as St Paul was on the Damascus road.

If the stories in the Gospels and the Acts of the Apostles, however some of the details are interpreted, are reliable evidence of the central truth of the resurrection of Jesus Christ, there are many consequences for the Christian. These are spelled out by St Paul in his letter to the Corinthians. Jesus was man and since by man came death, by man came also the resurrection of the dead (1 Cor. 15.21). In raising Christ from the dead, God acted in a way that affects the whole human race. The resurrection of Christ is the first-fruit of the resurrection of those who by faith are in Christ. The Easter hymn expresses this faith in simple and well known words:

> Jesus lives! Thy terrors now
> Can no longer, death, appal us.
> Jesus lives! By this we know
> Thou, O grave, canst not enthral us.

It is one thing to believe the resurrection of Jesus and to look at the stories of that past event; it is quite another thing to look ahead in expectation of our own resurrection. It is not enough that one man should have one opinion and a second person quite another opinion, as though Scriptures had nothing to tell us. There are indeed a number of guidelines in the New

Testament to guide and control our thinking.

First, there is the clear teaching that it is in Christ that there lies our hope. Since Adam represents our fallen and unredeemed human nature, man without Christ, St Paul is able to affirm, 'As in Adam all die, even so in Christ shall all be made alive.' Our hope of resurrection depends not only on the fact that Christ was raised from the dead. It does depend on this, as St Paul argues: 'Now if Christ be preached that He rose from the dead, how say some among you that there is no resurrection of the dead? And if there be no resurrection of the dead, then is Christ not risen . . . . and if Christ be not raised, your faith is vain; ye are yet in your sins. Then they also which are fallen asleep in Christ are perished' (1 Cor. 15.12-18). It is not just because of Christ that we have hope of resurrection, but also 'in Christ' that we have this hope. There is here that element of the uniqueness of Christ and even an element of exclusiveness of the Christian, which may cause offence to those who do not accept the Christian claim. It is necessary to ask in what lies their hope, when the Christian believes that God has given him 'a living hope by the resurrection of Jesus Christ from the dead' (1 Peter 1.3). According to the record of the Fourth Gospel, this follows from the teaching of Jesus himself. 'He that heareth my word, and believeth on Him that sent me, hath everlasting life and shall not come into condemnation; but is passed from death unto life' (John 5.24). Again, in the context of the feeding of the five thousand, Jesus is recorded as saying, 'This is the will of Him that sent me, that everyone that seeth the Son and believeth on him, may have everlasting life; and I will raise him up at the last day' (John 6.40). The theme is continued in the teaching about eating the Bread of Life. This is but one further illustration of the teaching that Christ shared our human life (and death) and invites us to share his life which has overcome death. In Adam we die — in Christ we are made alive.

The second point follows from the same thought. We can begin to share that divine life now; we do not have to wait for the death of our body. If we are in Christ, we already have that life which death cannot touch. We draw our life from him as surely as a branch draws its life from a vine of which it is a part; we lose that life if we are cut off from the source of life, as surely as a branch cut off from the source of which it was a part (John 15.1-7). In quite a different context, St Paul expresses the same thought. 'I am crucified with Christ, nevertheless I live; yet not I, but Christ liveth in me; and the life which I now live in the flesh, I live by the faith of the Son of God who loved me and gave Himself for me' (Gal. 2.20). Abiding in Christ gives us a new status as sons of God, which worldly death cannot touch. Indeed, for the Christian, life, death and resurrection are not so much a matter of physical state but of divine status. We cannot now know the physical properties which belonged to the body of the risen Christ; but we can accept that in life, in death, and in resurrection we can be with and in Christ. 'Where I am, there ye may be also' (John 14.3). At the practical level, this thought, anticipated by the psalmist, has been the strength of many at the time of earthly death. 'Yea, though I walk through the valley of the shadow of death, I will fear no evil; for Thou art with me' (Ps. 23.4). Our resurrection life will be life eternally with Christ; if we love him, that will be heaven.

The third fact of the resurrection life about which the Scriptures give us some guidance is that we shall have some means of expression. 'God giveth us a body, as it hath pleased Him' (1 Cor. 15.38). St Paul follows this assertion with argument and analogy, in the course of which he is making the point that the resurrection body is not the same as that frail body which is subject to earthly ills. 'Flesh and blood cannot inherit the Kingdom of God; neither doth corruption inherit incorruption' (1 Cor. 15.50). We do not sow the body that shall be but, as it were, bare grain. When grain is sown it dies and what grows from it is something new. Of necessity, all metaphors get mixed in trying to describe the indescribable, and St Paul's arguments are no exception. Equally, we cannot understand or describe the resurrection body of Jesus, so different in its properties from the body of flesh, yet a means of self-expression sufficient to enable the disciples to know that the person whom they encountered after Easter was the same person whom they had followed in trust before the Crucifixion. We cannot now know in what way we shall 'recognize' one another in life after death. However, it would follow from what has already been said that death cannot touch what is Christlike, and so it would be reasonable that we shall 'see' or recognize what in one another is of Christ. In so far as we are in Christ, that is all we shall want to see or recognize.

Just as in the resurrection of Jesus Christ there is emphasis in the Scriptures that it was the same person who died who also rose from the dead, so it

E

will be ourselves who will be raised. Analogies break
down at this point if they are taken too literally, but
death is not to be imagined as an impenetrable barrier.
Something happened to death when Christ accepted
it; he broke its power. In him that which is on one
side of death is united with that on the other. As
those who are in Christ comprise the Body of Christ,
so on both sides of the curtain of death they are one
body. We do not cease to be members of the family
of God, or the Body of Christ, just because our earthly
bodies happen to die. This unity of the Church here
and those of it the other side of death is what is
enshrined in the thought of the Communion of Saints.
We are not only compassed about with a great cloud
of witnesses; we are one with them in Christ. Thus we
find our unity with them by keeping close to Christ,
in whom they also live and move and have their being,
and not by any other means. There is one Body of
Christ only (one Lord, one faith, one baptism, one
God and Father of all). One practical consequence is
that when the Church celebrates a Saint's day, it is
commemorating not just a hero of the past (as seen
from our viewpoint in space-time) but rejoicing in the
fellowship of a fellow-member. To say that there is
continuity, as though the Church could be compared
with an iceberg, part of which is in the sunshine and
part submerged in the darkness of the ocean, might
be misleading or misconstrued. To say there is no
continuity, as though the veil had never been rent by
Christ, would be untrue.

Finally, we are taught in the Scripture that the life
beyond death is a life to which we can look forward
with joyful hope. The things that mar this life, some

of which are the consequences of the limitations of space-time and some of which are the consequences of human sin, ignorance, or frailty, will be at an end. There will be an end of hunger and thirst, and all that those two words represent. There shall be an end of tears and weeping (Rev. 7.16-17). Again, in the picture-language describing the New Jerusalem, the writer affirms that 'then God will wipe away all tears . . . and there shall be no more death, neither sorrow, nor crying, neither shall there be any more pain; for the former things are passed away' (Rev. 21.4). The imagery of angels and harps and crystal may not be attractive to everyone (though the possibility of silence for the space of half an hour might be attractive to some!), but the idea of constant praise expresses the idea of undiluted love; for praise is the language of love. It also expresses that peace of which harmony is the language. With love and peace, there will be nothing but joy.

All these things follow from the fundamental assertion that Christ became like us, one of us, that we might become like him, one in him. He shared our mortal life that we might share his divine life in eternity, a life over which death has no dominion. Because I live, ye shall live also. To enter that life during his earthly pilgrimage is the hope of every sincere Christian. It is truly a matter of life and death. He that hath the Son hath life; he that hath not the Son hath not life.